Ukulele Picking Tunes

BEAUTIFUL AIRS AND BALLADS OF THE BRITISH ISLES

Ondřej Šárek

Mahogany All Solid Concert Ukulele MAS-C cover image courtesy of Lanikai Ukuleles.

WWW.MELBAY.COM

Preface

The ukulele can be such a lyrical instrument. I have always loved hearing beautiful ballads performed on the ukulele. This book presents 23 beautiful airs and ballads of the British Isles scored for soprano ukulele solo. Traditional airs, love songs, songs of home and longing as well as compositions of the great Irish harpist, Turlough O'Carolan make up the collection. I've also included arrangements of a number of original airs by William Bay.

All of the solos are presented in notation and tablature with back-up chords included. I have included fingering where appropriate.

I hope you enjoy the mystic beauty of these marvelous airs and ballads.

Ondřej Šárek

Index of Tunes

An Drochshaol

The Hard Times

Adagio ♩ = 88

William Bay

25
25
C
31
31
37
37
D
43
43

The Galway Shawl

Freely, No set tempo ♩ = 80

Believe Me, If All Those Endearing Young Charms

Lyrically ♩ = 94

C

Down by the Sally Gardens

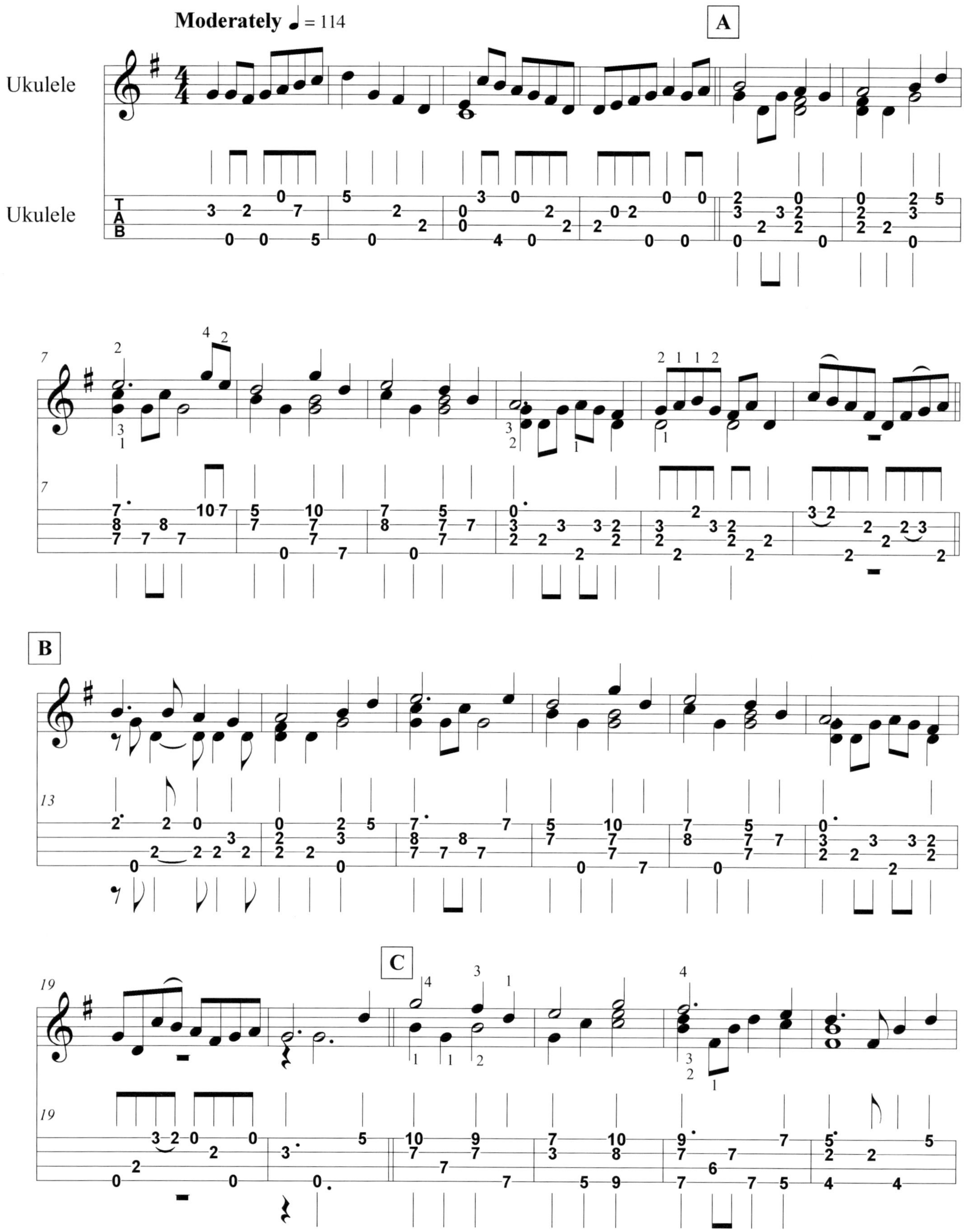

D
E

Fields of Culloden

William Bay

Lento ♩ = 84

D
E

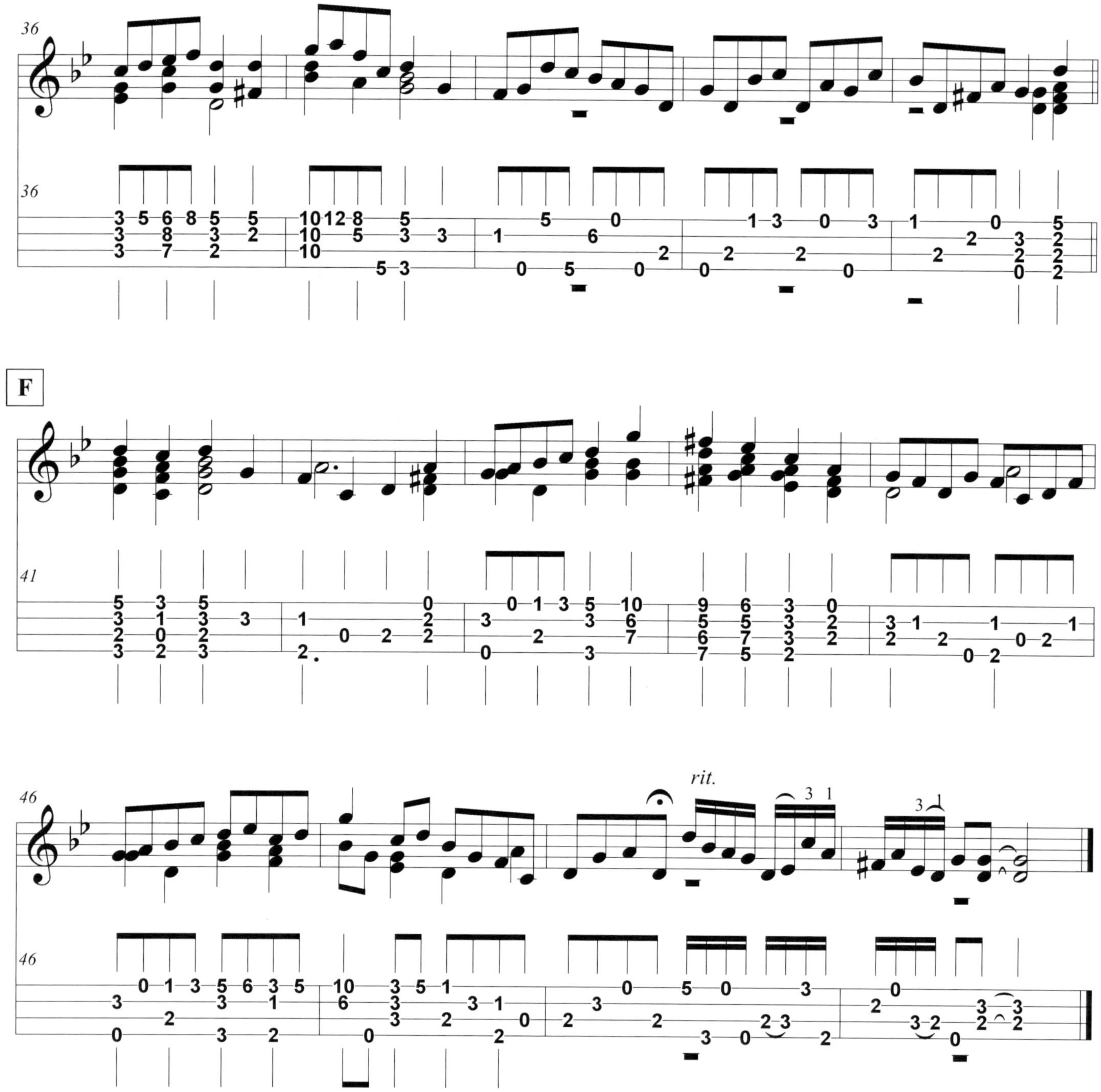
36
F
41
46
rit.

Star of the County Down

C
D

rit.

Call the Ewes

C

Fair Flower of Northumberland

rit.

I Went to Visit the Roses

C
rit.

Irish Prayer

Peacefully ♩ = 80

William Bay

D
21
26
31

Jock O'Hazeldean

Slowly and Lyrically ♩ = 120

John Anderson, My Jo

Slowly ♩ = 74

Cailin Deas Crúite na mBó

Pretty Girl Milking Her Cow

Freely ♩ = 92

26
C
33
40
47

Scarborough Fair

24
29
C
34
rit.
39

She Moved Through the Fair

Sheebeg and Sheemor

Turlough O'Carolan

Moderately ♩ = 96

C

The Flowers of Sweet Erin the Green

C

The Marsh of Rhuddlan

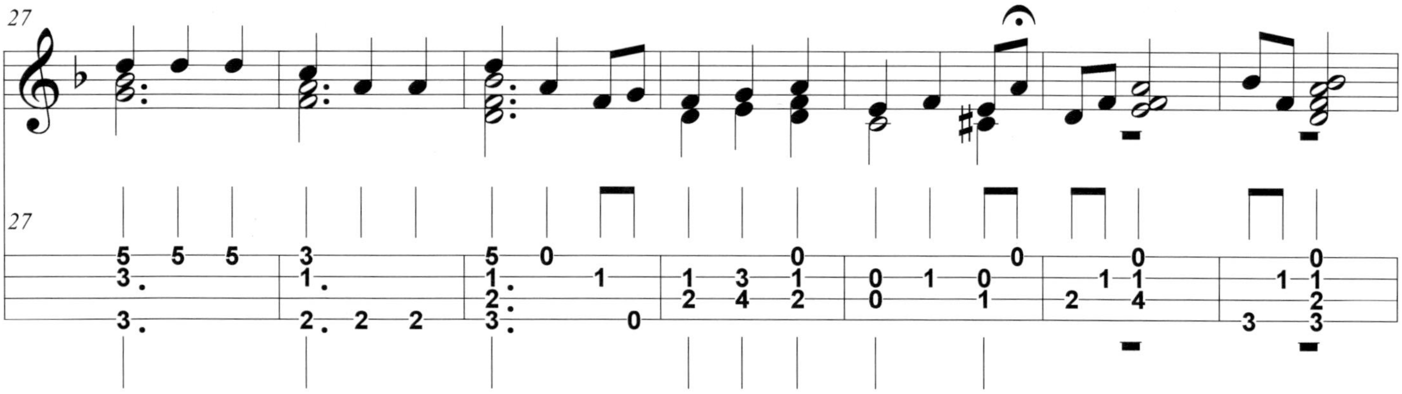
27

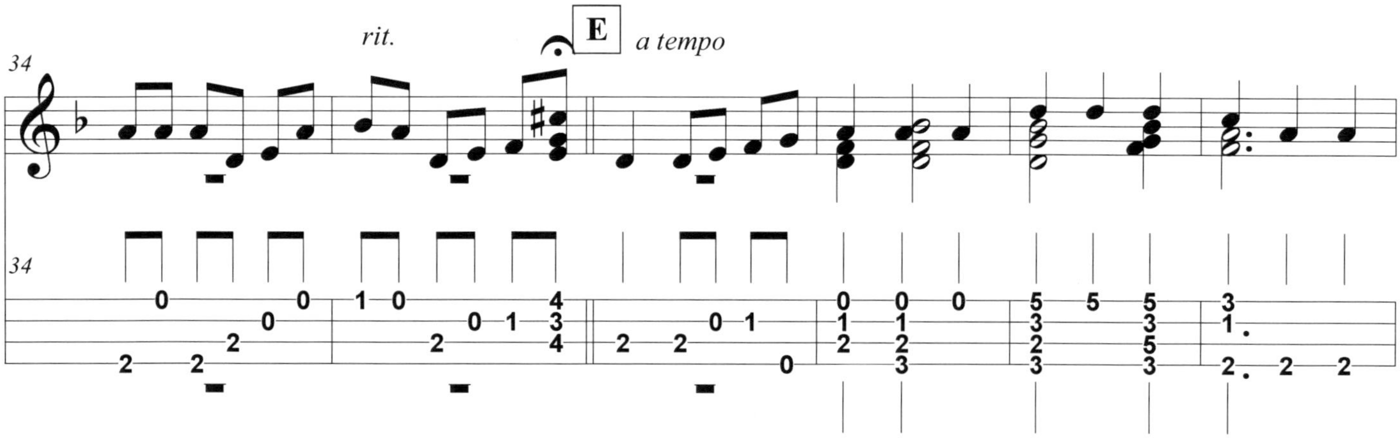
34
rit.
E
a tempo

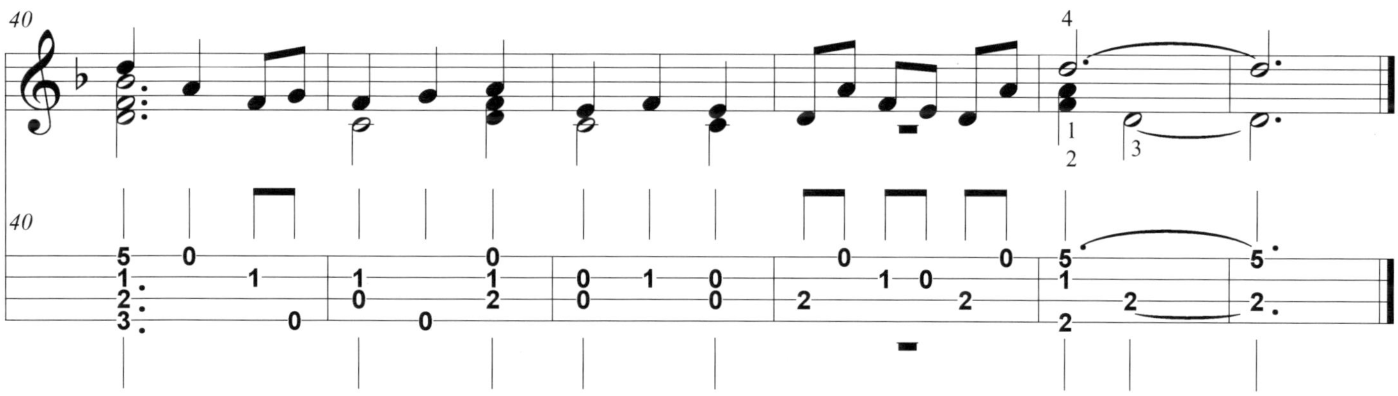
40

The Water Is Wide

Once I Had a Sweetheart

C
Slower
rit.

Wild Mountain Thyme

C

My Irish Home

William Bay

Larghetto ♩ = 64

B
C

The Shearing's Not for You

Scottish

Other Mel Bay Ukulele Books